Alphabet, Colors, Numbers, Shapes

Table Of Contents

Alphabet
Learning the letters A, a 4
Learning the letters B, b 5
Learning the letters C, c 6
Learning the letters D, d 7
Learning the letters E, e 8
Learning the letters F, f 9
Learning the letters G, g 10
Learning the letters H, h 11
Learning the letters I, i 12
Learning the letters J, j 13
Learning the letters K, k 14
Learning the letters L, l 15
Learning the letters M, m 16
Learning the letters N, n 17
Learning the letters O, o 18
Learning the letters P, p 19
Learning the letters Q, q 20
Learning the letters R, r 21
Learning the letters S, s 22
Learning the letters T, t 23
Learning the letters U, u 24
Learning the letters V, v 25
Learning the letters W, w 26
Learning the letters X, x 27
Learning the letters Y, y 28
Learning the letters Z, z 29
Saying the alphabet 30
Writing the alphabet 31
Writing the letters A-I 32
Writing the letters J-R 33
Writing the letters S-Z 34
Writing the letters a-i 35
Writing the letters j-r 36
Writing the letters s-z 37

Numbers
Recognizing the number 1 38
Recognizing the number 2 39
Recognizing the number 3 40
Recognizing the number 4 41
Recognizing the number 5 42
Recognizing the number 6 43
Recognizing the number 7 44
Recognizing the number 8 45
Recognizing the number 9 46
Recognizing the number 10 47
Matching numbers to number words 48

Recognizing number words 49
Recognizing number words 50
Counting-numbers 1-5 51
Counting-numbers 1-5 52
Counting-numbers 1-5 53
Counting-numbers 1-5 54
Counting-numbers 1-5 55
Counting-numbers 1-5 56
Counting-numbers 6-10 57
Counting-numbers 6-10 58
Counting-numbers 6-10 59
Counting-numbers 6-10 60
Counting-numbers 6-10 61
Counting-numbers 1-10 62
Counting-numbers 1-10 63
Writing numbers 1-5 64
Writing numbers 6-10 65
Sums through 4 66
Sums through 4 67

Colors
Learning the color red 68
Learning the color red 69
Learning the color red 70
Learning the color blue 71
Learning the color blue 72
Learning the color blue 73
Learning the color orange 74
Learning the color orange 75
Learning the color orange 76
Learning the color yellow 77
Learning the color yellow 78
Learning the color yellow 79
Learning the color green 80
Learning the color green 81
Learning the color brown 82
Learning the color brown 83
Learning the color black 84
Learning the color black 85
Learning the color pink 86
Color review-red, blue, yellow 87
Color review-green, purple, orange 88
Color review-black, brown, gray 89
Reading color words 90
Reading color words 91
Reading color words 92
Reading color words 93

Reading color words 94

Shapes
Tracing a circle/ writing the word "circle" 95
Tracing circles 96
Recognizing a circle 97
Cutting and pasting circles 98
Tracing a square/writing the word "square" 99
Tracing squares 100
Recognizing squares 101
Recognizing squares 102
Tracing a rectangle/writing the word "rectangle" 103
Tracing rectangles 104
Recognizing rectangles 105
Recognizing rectangles 106
Tracing a triangle/ writing the word "triangle" 107
Tracing triangles 108
Cutting and pasting triangles 109
Recognizing triangles 110
Shapes review 111
Shapes review 112
Shapes review 113
Tracing a heart/writing the word "heart" 114
Tracing hearts 115
Tracing a diamond/writing the word "diamond" 116
Tracing diamonds 117
Tracing an oval/writing the word "oval" 118
Tracing ovals 119
Tracing a star/writing the word "star" 120
Tracing stars 121
Shapes review 122
Shapes review 123
Shapes review 124

Awards
Alphabet/colors 125
Numbers/ Shapes 126
Badges 127
Certificate 128

Kelley Wingate products are available at fine educational supply stores throughout the U. S. and Canada.

Beginning Skills CD-3701   Printed in the United States Of America ISBN 0-88724-419-X

Ready-To-Use Ideas and Activities

Learning the basic skills are children's building blocks for understanding more complex concepts. The stronger their foundation is in the basics, the easier they will be able to progress through harder tasks.

The alphabet, colors, numbers, and shapes are some of the first skills children must master before they can move on to more challenging activities. Learning these can be fun for everyone.

Remember as you read through the following activities, and as you go through this book, that all children learn at their own rate, that repetition is important, and that it is critical to help children build self esteem by building their self-confidence and helping them be successful.

If you are working with a child at home, try to set up a quiet comfortable environment where you will work. Make it a special time to which you each look forward. Do only a few activities at a time. Try to end each session on a positive note. Remember that building self-esteem and confidence goes hand in hand with successful learning.

• The back of this book contains removable flash cards that will be great to use for basic skill and enrichment activities. Pull the flash cards out and either cut them apart or if you have access to a paper cutter use it to cut the flash cards apart. There are six blank flash cards that may be used as replacement cards if any are lost or you may make up six more flash cards that would be appropriate for the child/children using this book.

The following are just a few ideas on ways that you may use the flash cards.

• Take the 26 capital letter flash cards. Have the children put them in alphabetical order. After you are done, sing the alphabet song. If the children do not know the entire alphabet yet, start with just a few of the letters and keep adding to them until the child/children can recognize all of the letters.

• Take the 26 lowercase flash cards. Have the children put them in alphabetical order. Talk about the upper and lowercase letters. Which ones

CD-3701

look alike and which ones look different? What sounds do each of the letters make?

• Leave all of the lowercase flash cards face up. Take the uppercase letter flash cards and turn them over so that they are picture side up. Mix the pictures up; then take them one at a time and see if the children can match the picture to the correct lowercase letter. They may check their answer by flipping the picture word over and seeing if they have the capital letter that matches the lowercase letter that is showing.

• Take both sets of number flash cards and have the child/children put them in numerical order from 0 to 10. Next, take the cards that have the number words on them and see if the children can match the number word with the numeric symbol or numeral. Once they can do that, try playing concentration by matching the number word to the numeral.

• Put the number flash cards out in order. Take a bag of beans or a set of counters. See if the children can put the correct number of beans or counters in front of each number card. Another great activity involves writing the number "15" on a blank flash card. See if the child/children can count to "15" and if they can count out the correct number of beans. Try "20", "30", "40", and "50".

• Take the color and shape flash cards. Take each (black & white) shape flash cards one at a time, look at it, identify it, and talk about it. For example, talk about the circle flash card. Where else do you see circles around you everyday; coins, tires on cars, the sun, many knobs on TV sets and other electronic equipment, etc. The oval is not as common but you do see it in an egg or in a picture of how the earth rotates around the sun. Can the children think of any other shapes? There are some other really interesting shapes like a rhombus (an equilateral parallelogram), a pentagon, an octagon, a parallelogram, or trapezoid.

Ready-To-Use Ideas and Activities

Take the set of colored shape flash cards and the black and white ones and see if the children can match the black and white shape to the correct colored shape. This could be a great way to start a discussion on attributes. For example, we have two cards that have squares on them. They are alike in that both are squares. They are different because one is brown and the other is not.

Leave the black & white set of shape cards face up and turn the colored set, which has the shape word written on them, word side up. See if the children can sound out the shape word. Talk about the words and then see if they can match the word with the correct picture.

• Take the colored shape flash cards and see if the children can tell you what color each shape is. Talk about the colors. Where in their everyday life do they see these colors and what other colors do they see. Take the flash cards that have the color words written on them in color and have the child/children match the color word to the correct colored shape.

1. Color the upper case A and the lower case a.

2. Color each apple red if it has an A.
   Color each apple green if it has an a.

CD-3701

1. Color the upper case B and the lower case b.

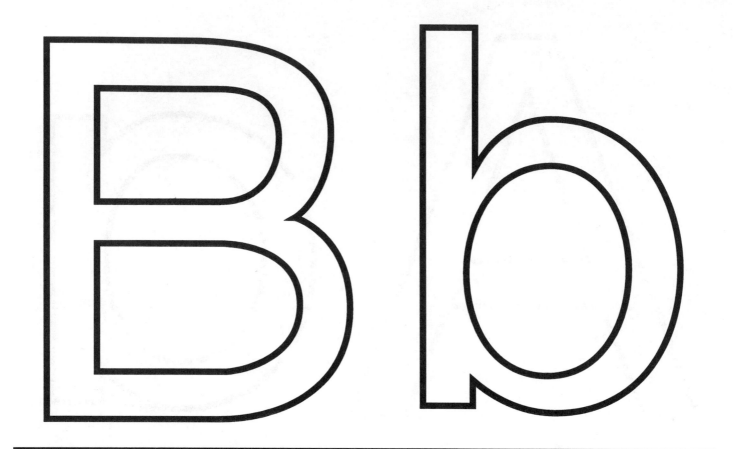

2. Color each balloon if it has a B or b.

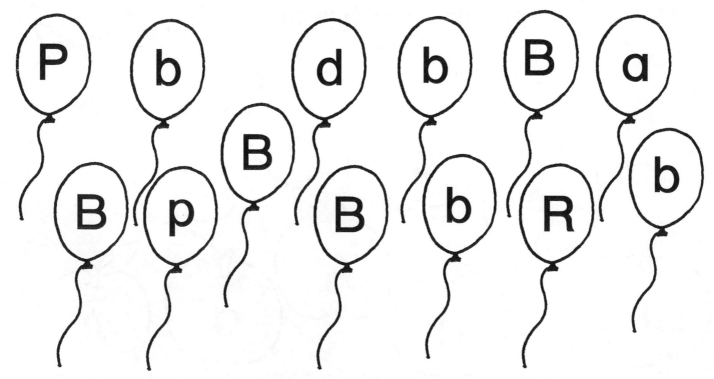

5

CD-3701

1. Color the upper case C and the lower case c.

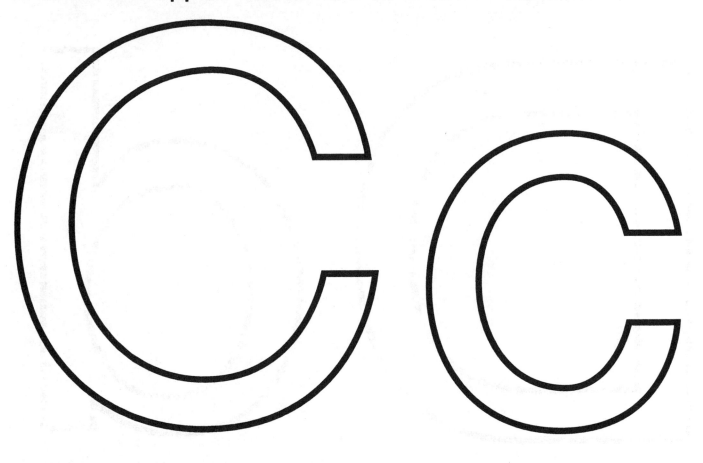

2. Find all of the candies with a C or c. Color them red.

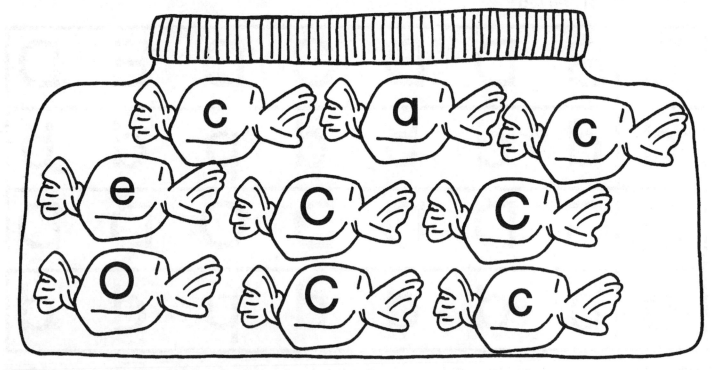

1. Color the upper case D and the lower case d.

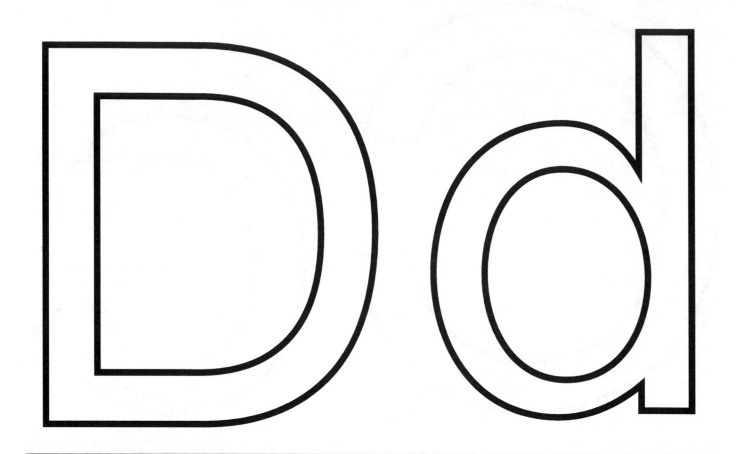

2. In each row circle the letters that are the same as the first letter.

D	B	D	D	C	D	E	D
d	d	d	b	d	p	d	b
D	G	D	D	D	O	D	D
d	b	d	d	d	p	d	d

7   CD-3701

1. Color the upper case E and the lower case e.

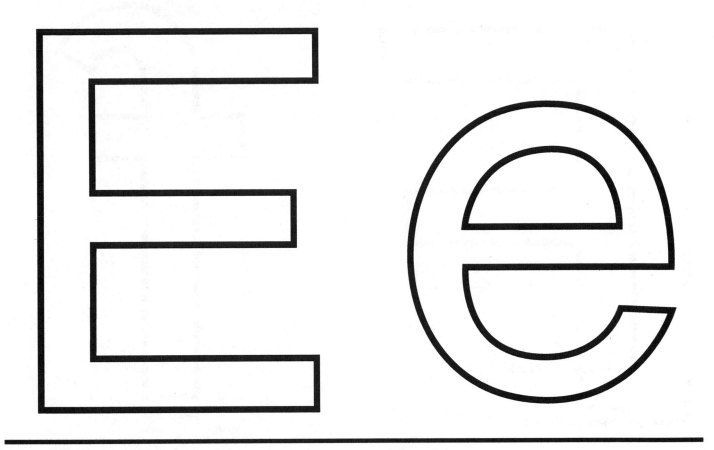

2. Color each space green if it has an E or e.
   Color all of the other spaces purple.

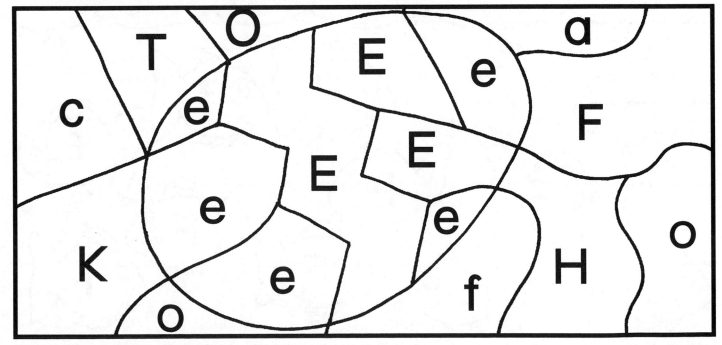

8   CD-3701

1. Color the upper case F and the lower case f.

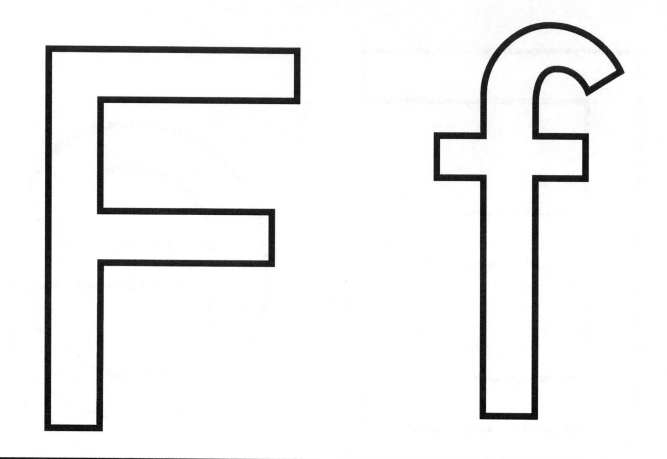

2. Color each fish green if it has an F.
   Color each fish blue if it has an f.

CD-3701

1. Color the upper case G and the lower case g.

2. Draw a line from each G or g to the girl.

1. Color the upper case H and the lower case h.

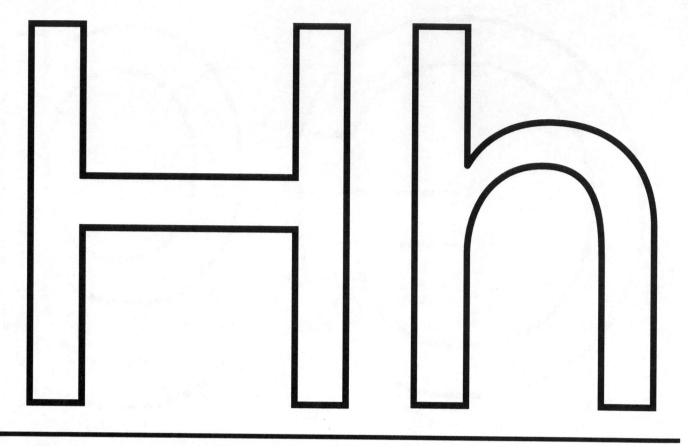

2. Draw a line from each H or h to the hat.

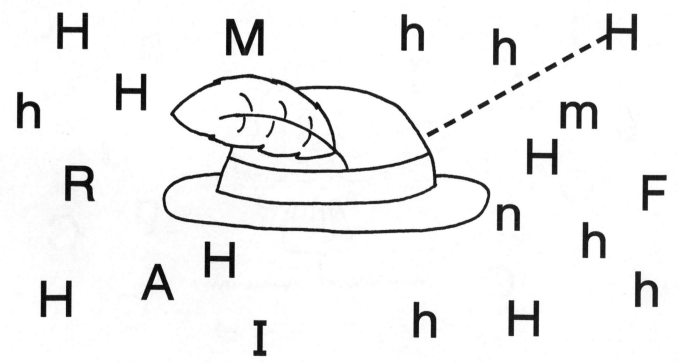

1. Color the upper case I and the lower case i.

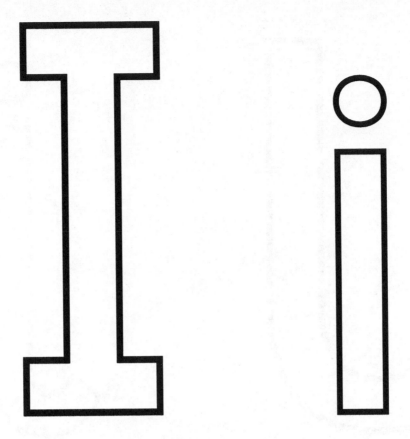

2. Color each ice cube if it has an I or i.

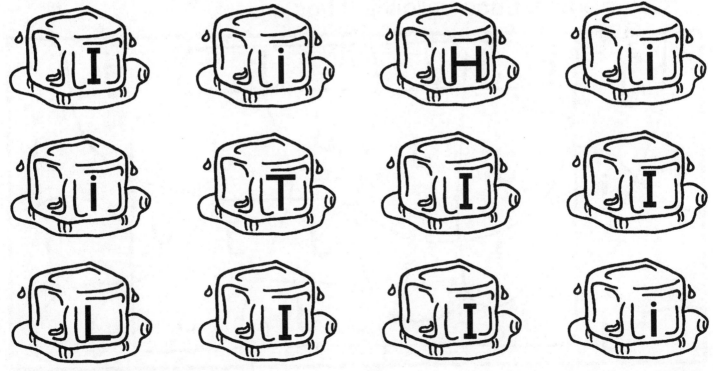

1. Color the upper case J and the lower case j.

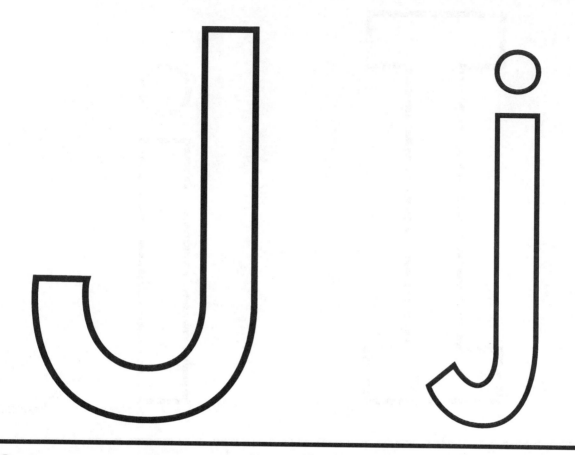

2. Color each space blue if it has a J.
   Color each space yellow if it has a j.

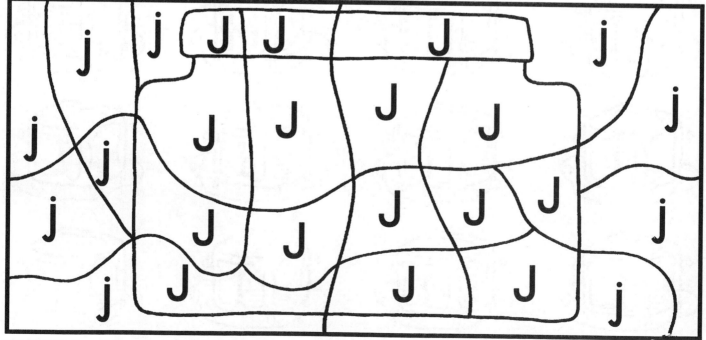

13

CD-3701

1. Color the upper case K and the lower case k.

2. In each row circle the letters that are the same as the first letter.

K	B	K	K	H	K	K	R
k	b	x	k	k	v	k	k
K	K	K	K	X	Z	K	Y
k	k	d	k	k	t	b	k

       CD-3701

1. Color the upper case L and the lower case l.

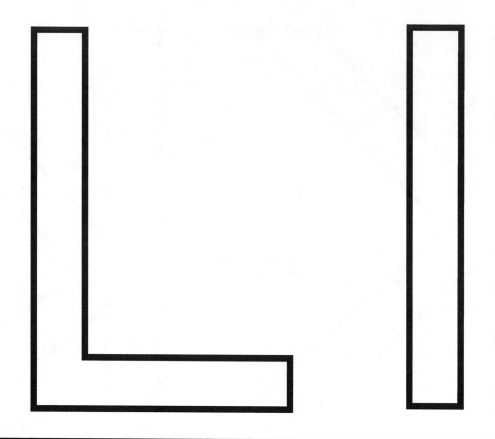

2. Color each space green if it has an L or l.

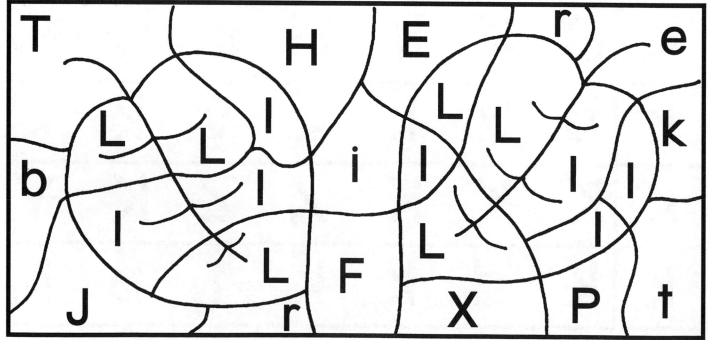

1. Color the upper case M and the lower case m.

2. Color each space yellow if it has an M or m.

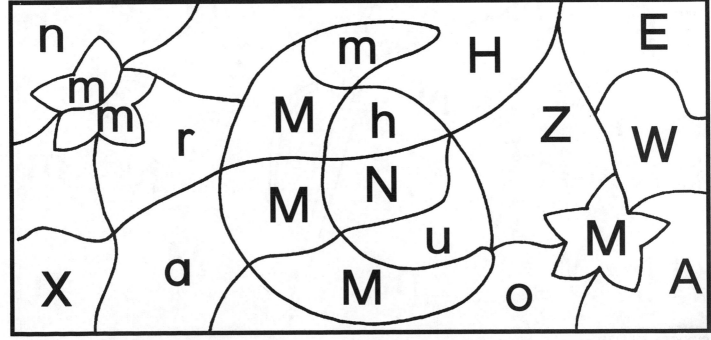

16

CD-3701

1. Color the upper case N and the lower case n.

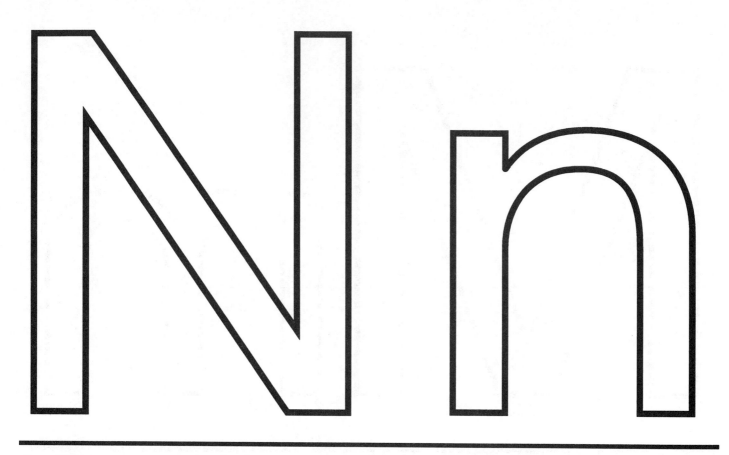

2. Draw a line from each N or n to the needle.

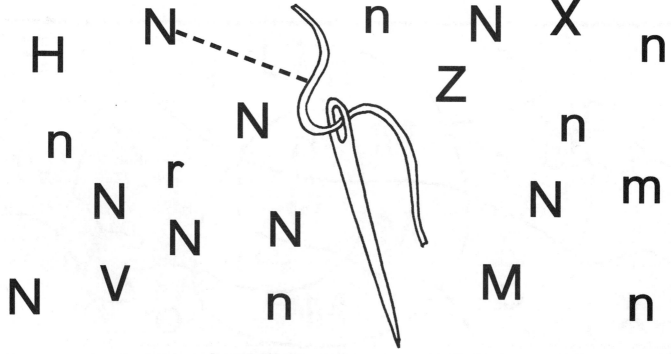

I. Color the upper case O and the lower case o.

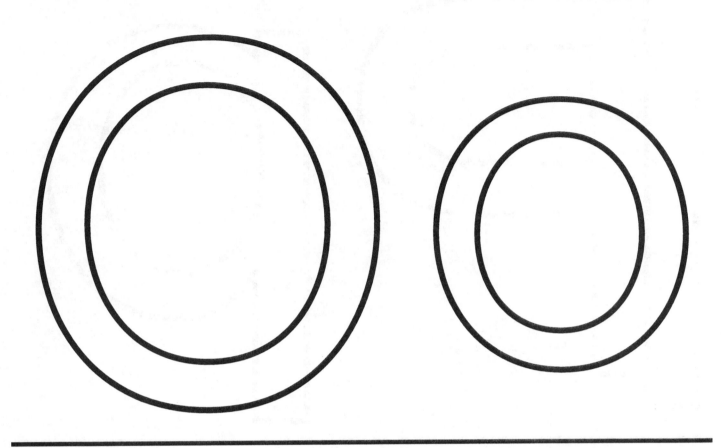

2. In each row circle the letters that are the same as the first letter.

O	O	O	G	O	D	O	C
O	Q	O	C	O	G	O	O
o	a	c	o	o	d	o	o
o	o	o	b	e	o	o	o

1. Color the upper case P and the lower case p.

2. Color each purse if it has a P or p.

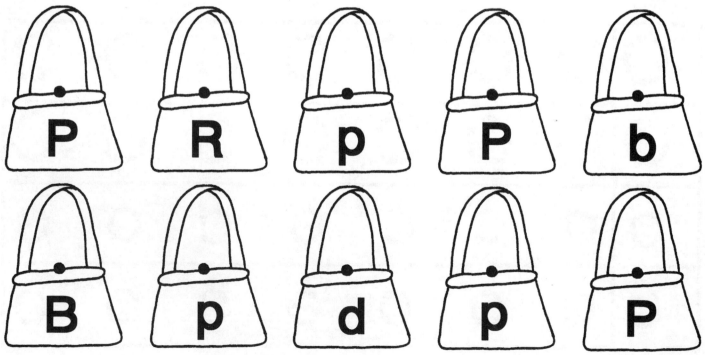

19

CD-3701

1. Color the upper case Q and the lower case q.

2. Finish this beautiful quilt by coloring each space pink if it has a Q or blue if it has a q.

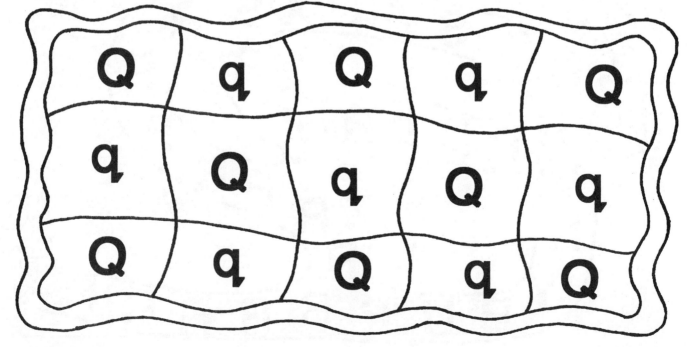

1. Color the upper case R and the lower case r.

2. Help the girl get to the ice cream by following the "R"s.

21

1. Color the upper case S and the lower case s.

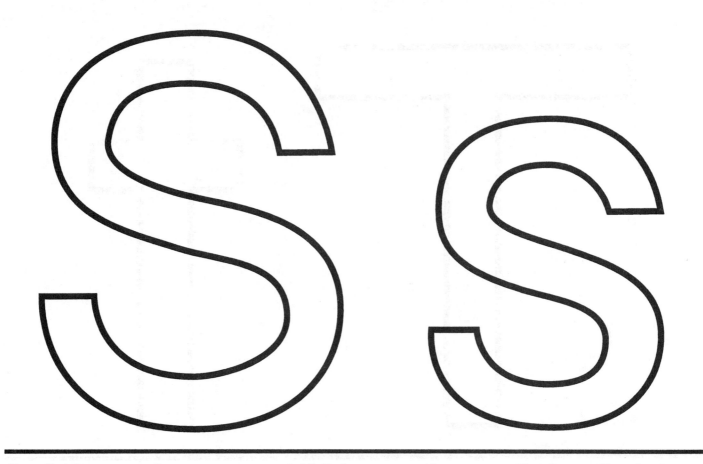

2. Color each space red if it has an S or s. Color all of the other spaces blue.

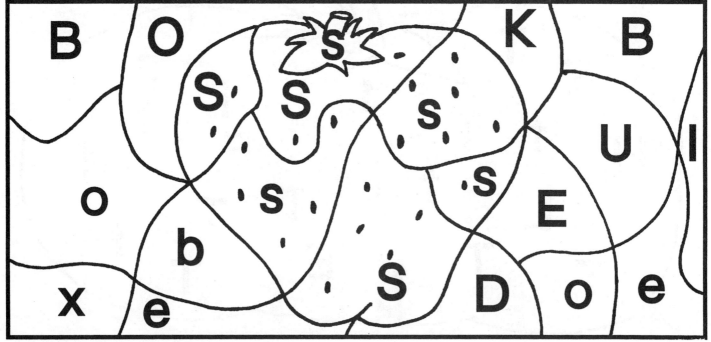

CD-3701

skill: recognizing the letter T, t

1. Color the upper case T and the lower case t.

2. Find and circle each T or t in the tomato.

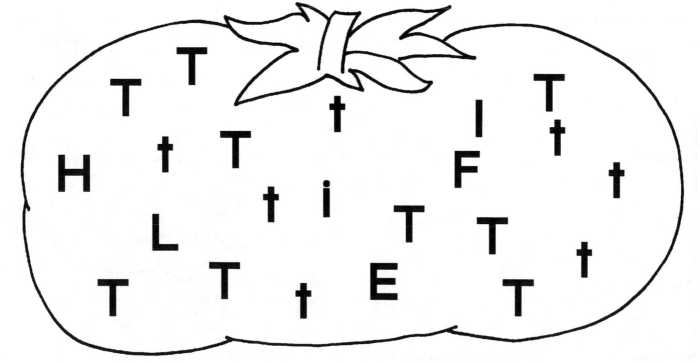

CD-3701

1. Color the upper case U and the lower case u.

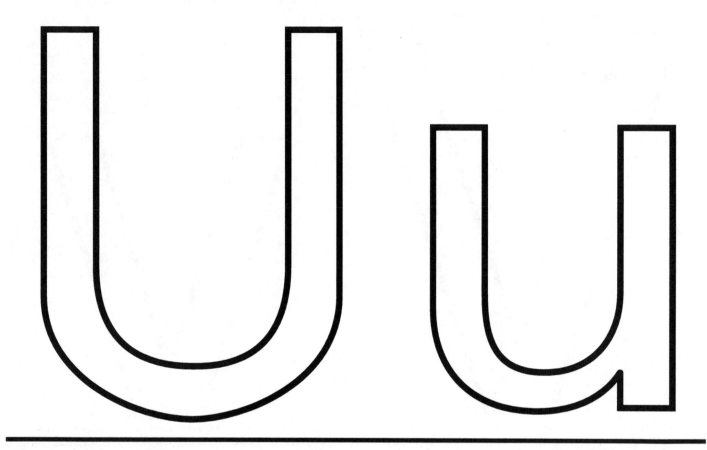

2. Color each rain drop purple if it has a U or orange if it has a u.

24

CD-3701

1. Color the upper case V and the lower case v.

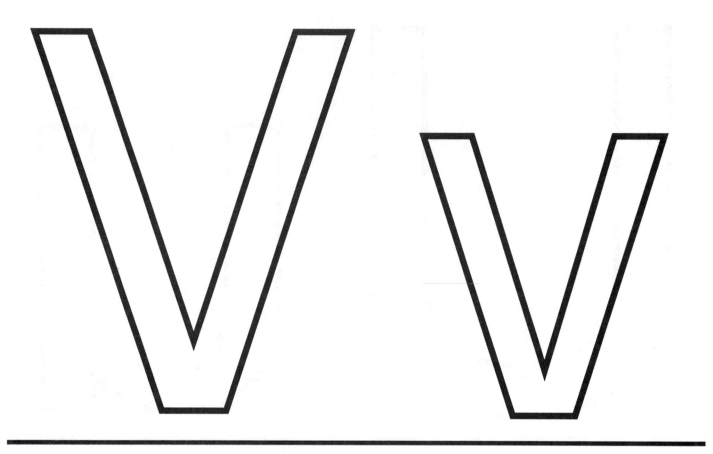

2. Color each vase that has a V or v.

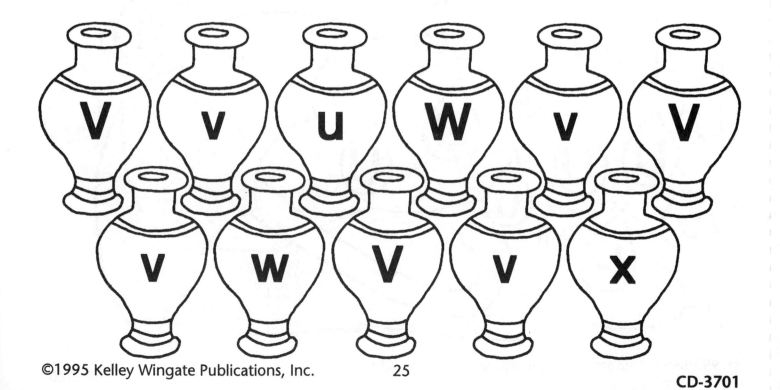

         CD-3701

1. Color the upper case W and the lower case w.

2. Draw a line from each W or w to the whale.

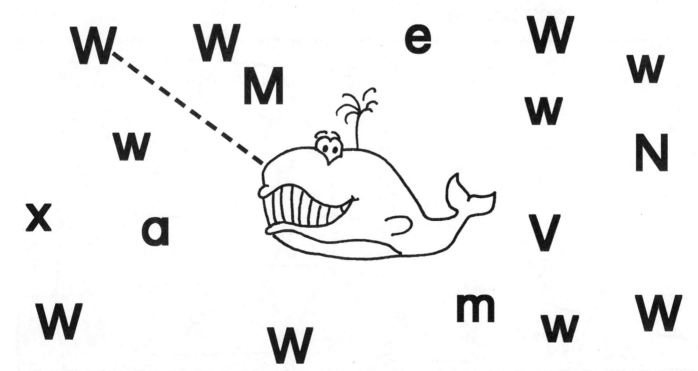

1. Color the upper case X and the lower case x.

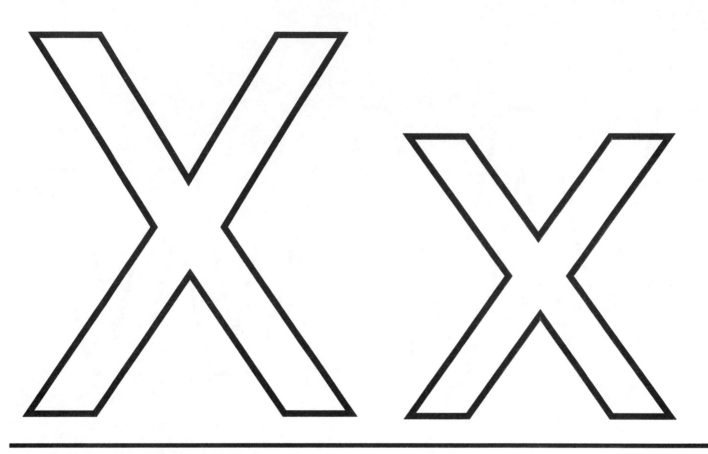

2. Color each space green if it has an X or x. Color all of the other spaces brown.

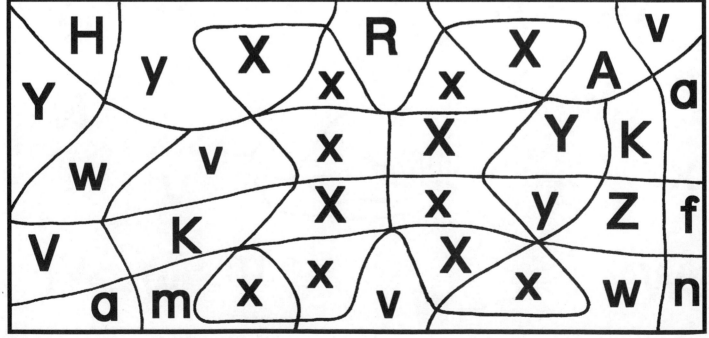

27   CD-3701

1. Color the upper case Y and the lower case y.

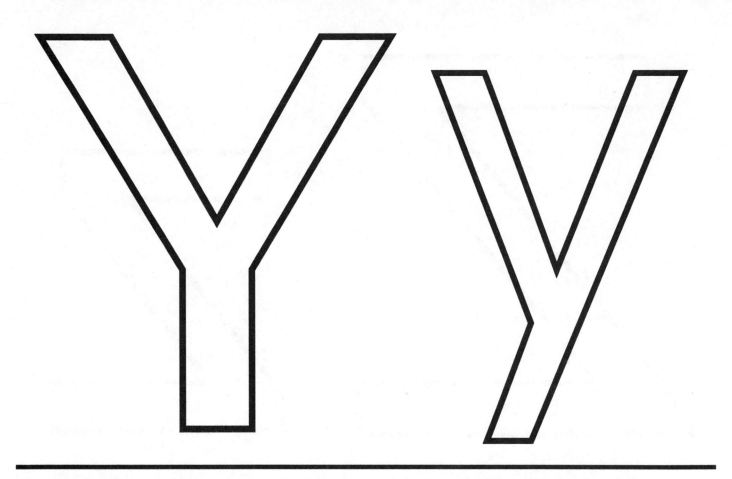

2. Help the bunny get to the carrot by following the Ys.

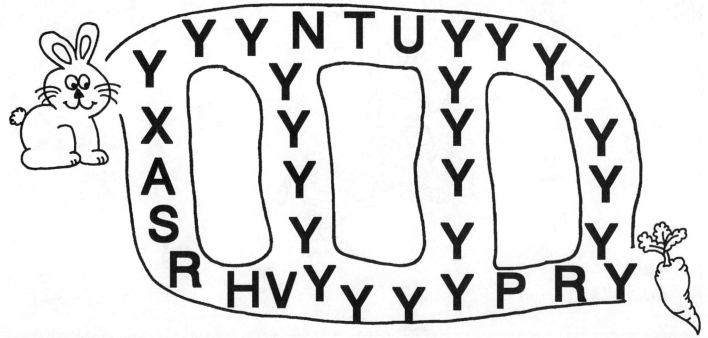

1. Color the upper case Z and the lower case z.

2. Draw a line from each Z or z to the zebra.

Name_____

skill: saying the alphabet

Practice saying the alphabet.

I think I can say all of these!!

A	B	C	D	E	F	G
H	I	J	K	L	M	N
O	P	Q	R	S	T	U
V	W	X	Y	Z		

a	b	c	d	e	f	g
h	i	j	k	l	m	n	o
p	q	r	s	t	u	v
w	x	y	z			

CD-3701

Name_____

Trace over the dotted lines to complete the letters.

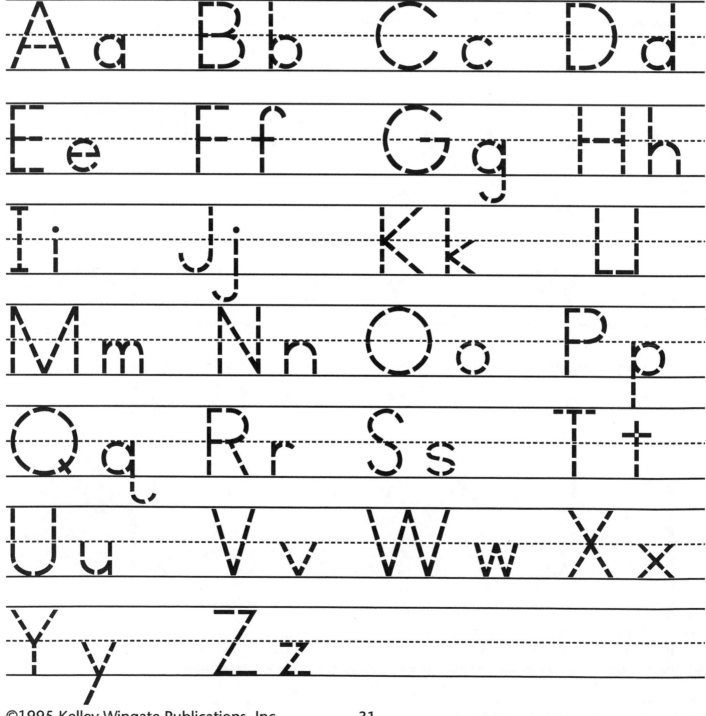

CD-3701

Name _____

Practice writing the letters.

A A A

B B B

C C C

D D D

E E E

F F F

G G G

H H H

I I I

CD-3701

Name _____

Practice writing the letters.

J J J J

K K K K

L L L L

M M M M

N N N N

O O O O

P P P P

Q Q Q Q

R R R R

CD-3701

Practice writing the letters.

S S S

T T T

U U U

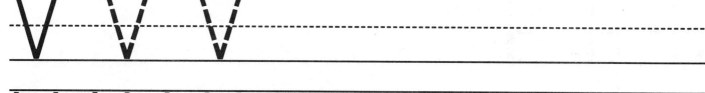

V V V

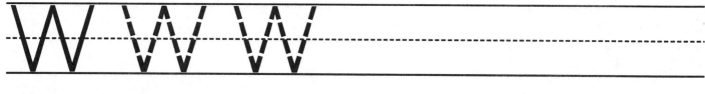

W W W

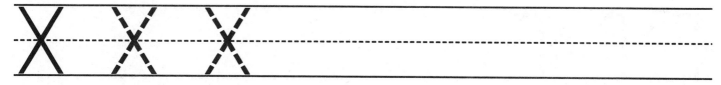

X X X

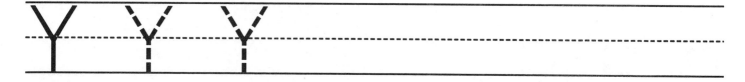

Y Y Y

Z Z Z

Name_____

Practice writing the letters.

a   a   a

b   b   b

c   c   c

d   d   d

e   e   e

f   f   f

g   g   g

h   h   h

i   i   i

Practice writing the letters.

j   j   j

k   k   k

l   l   l

m   m   m

n   n   n

o   o   o

p   p   p

q   q   q

r   r   r

CD-3701

Practice writing the letters.

S s s

t t t t

u u u u

v v v v

w w w w

x x x x

y y y y

z z z z

I. Color the number I.

2. Color this **one** happy shark.

CD-3701

1. Color the number 2.

2. Color these **two** friendly frogs.

39   CD-3701

1. Color the number 3.

2. Color these three smiling snails.

1. **Color the number 4.**

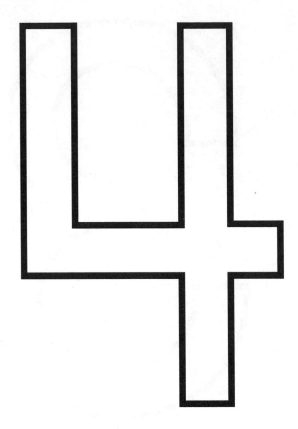

2. **Color these four funny fish.**

41

CD-3701

1. Color the number 5.

2. Color these **five** smiling stars.

42   CD-3701

1. Color the number 6.

---

2. Color these **six** beautiful butterflies.

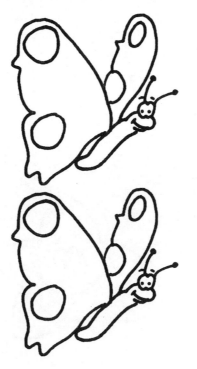
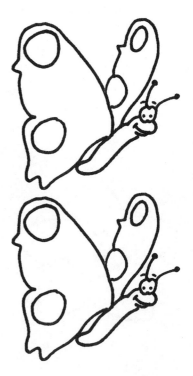

CD-3701

1. Color the number 7.

2. Color these **seven** batty bats.

    44   CD-3701

Name_____

1. Color the number 8.

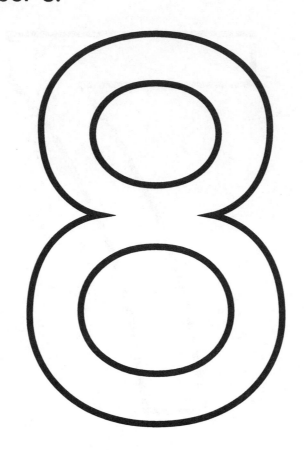

2. Color these eight portly pigs.

45   **CD-3701**

1. Color the number 9.

---

2. Count and color these **nine** big balloons.

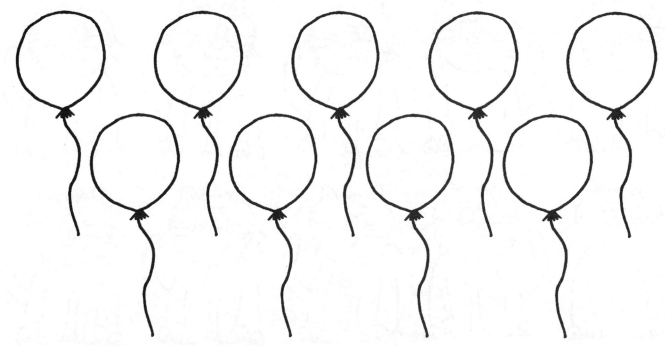

CD-3701

1. Color the number 10.

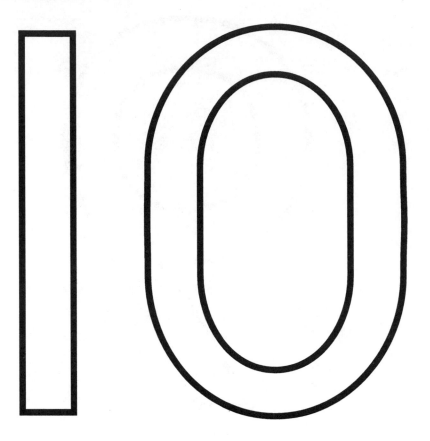

2. Count and color these **ten** cute cats.

CD-3701

Name _____

Draw a line to match each numeral to the correct number word.

0	two
1	one
2	five
3	eight
4	zero
5	three
6	nine
7	four
8	seven
9	six

(2 is connected to two with a dashed line)

Name_____

On each mitten write the correct numeral.

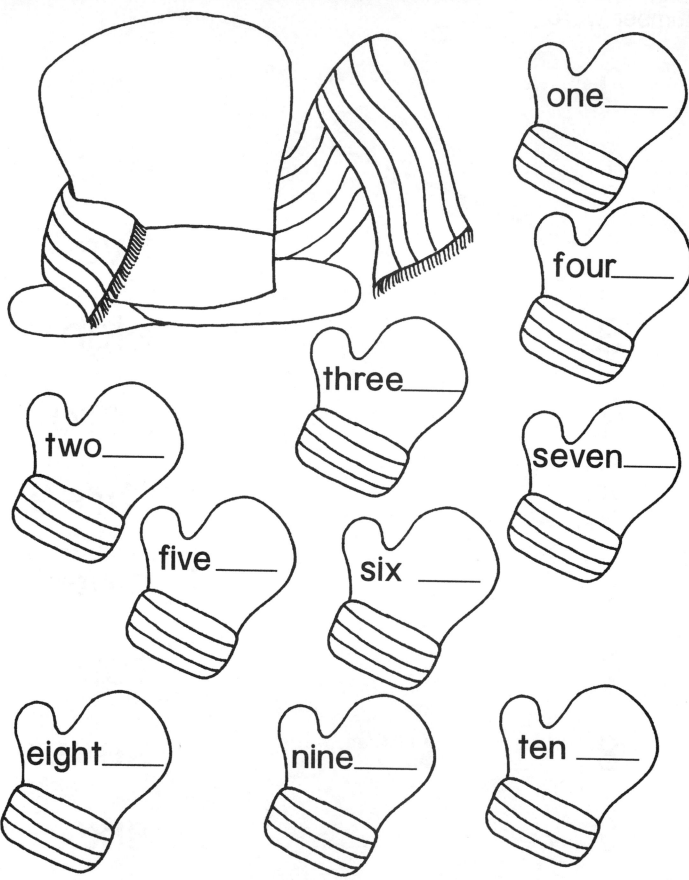

one_____

four_____

three_____

two_____

seven_____

five_____

six_____

eight_____

nine_____

ten_____

CD-3701

Name_____ skill: recognizing number words

On each cloud write the correct numeral.

one ____

three____

two____

four____

five ____

six ____

seven____

eight____

nine____

ten ____

CD-3701

Name _____

Count the number of objects in each row.
Circle the correct numeral.

| | 1 | 2 | 3 | 4 | 5 |

| | 1 | 2 | 3 | 4 | 5 |

| | 1 | 2 | 3 | 4 | 5 |

| | 1 | 2 | 3 | 4 | 5 |

| | 1 | 2 | 3 | 4 | 5 |

| | 1 | 2 | 3 | 4 | 5 |

CD-3701

Name _____

Count the number of objects in each row.
Circle the correct numeral.

			1	2	3	4	5
tree	tree	tree	1	2	3	4	5
hamburger	hamburger		1	2	3	4	5
tomato			1	2	3	4	5
keys			1	2	3	4	5
cactus			1	2	3	4	5
bones			1	2	3	4	5

52   CD-3701

In each row color the correct number of objects.

2

3

5

1

4

53

skill: counting numbers 1-5

In each row color the correct number of objects.

3

2

4

5

1

CD-3701

Name_____

Match each vase to the correct number of flowers.

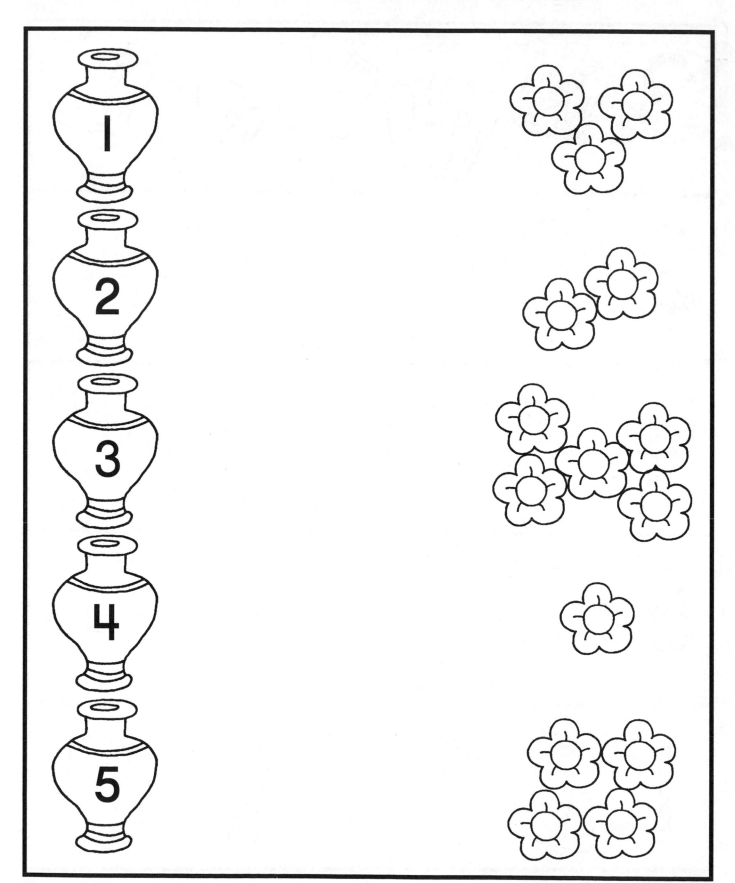

Name_____ Skill: counting

Count the number of objects in each row.
Write the numeral in the blank.

 ___shoes

 ___fish

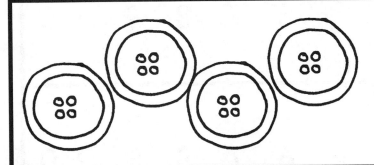 ___buttons

  ___hamburgers

 ___tomato

Name _____

Count the number of objects in each row.
Circle the correct numeral.

	6 7 8 9 10
	6 7 8 9 10
	6 7 8 9 10
	6 7 8 9 10
	6 7 8 9 10
	6 7 8 9 10

CD-3701

Count the number of objects in each row.
Circle the correct numeral.

6 7 8 9 10

6 7 8 9 10

6 7 8 9 10

6 7 8 9 10

6 7 8 9 10

6 7 8 9 10

In each row color the correct number of objects.

7

9

10

6

8

Name_____

In each row color the correct number of objects.

8

9

7

10

6

Name_____

Match each bean pod to the correct number of beans.

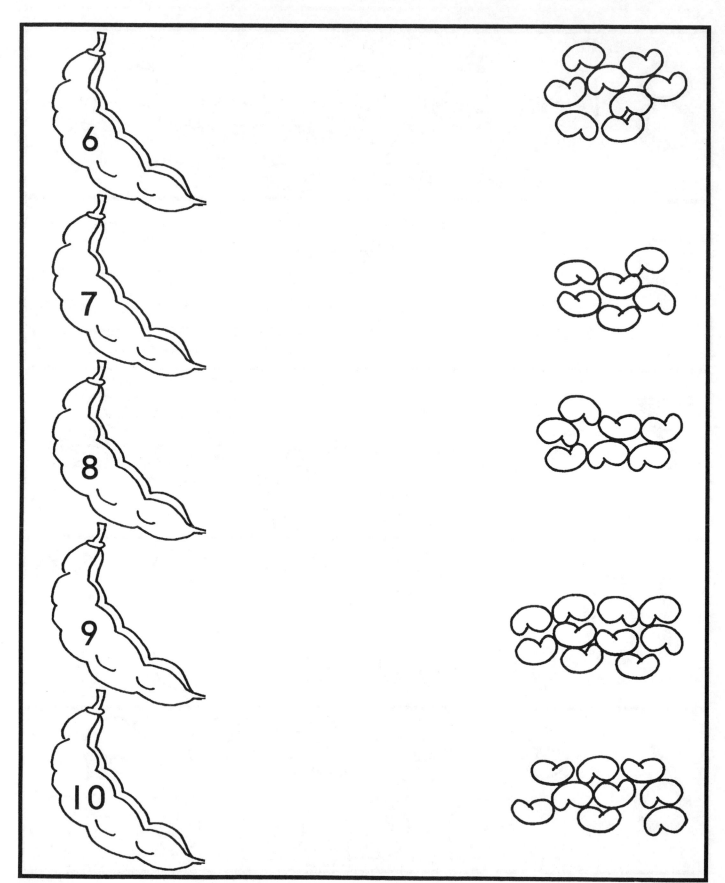

CD-3701

Name_____

In each gum machine draw the correct number of gumballs.

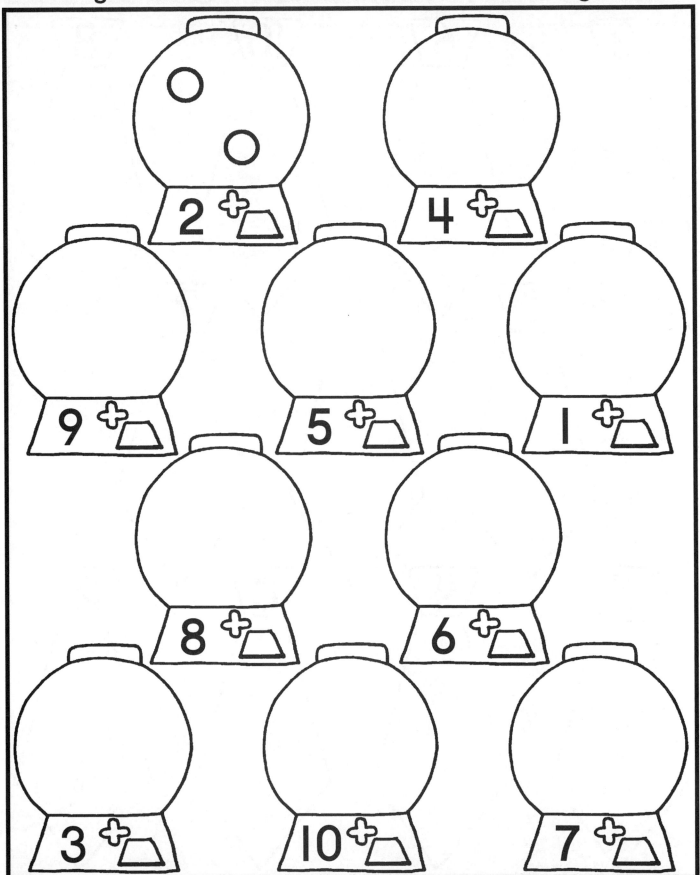

Name_____

On each tie draw the correct number of dots.

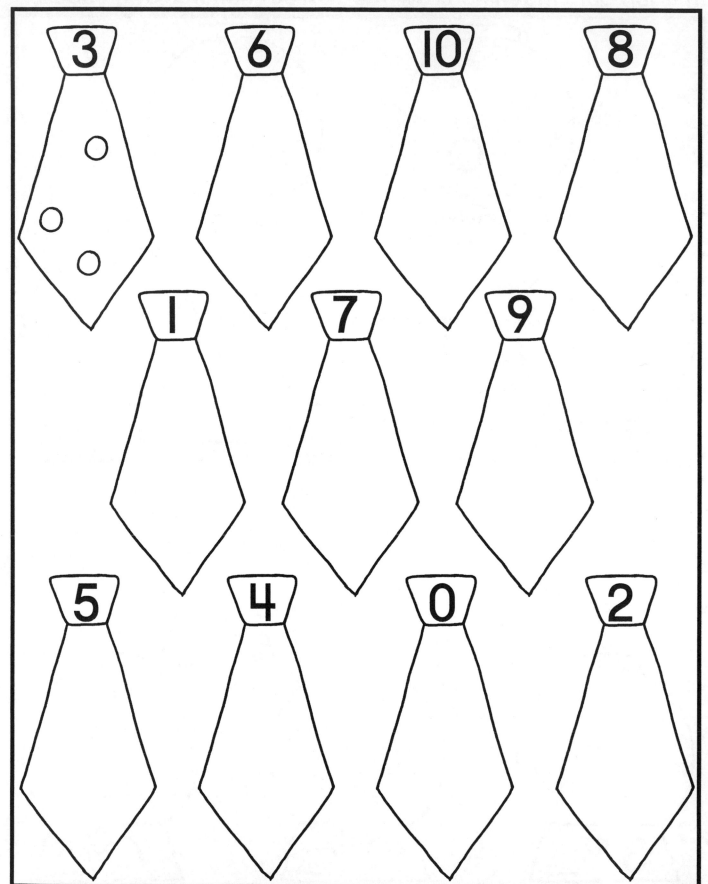

CD-3701

Practice writing each numeral.

Take your time!!

1 1 1

2 2 2

3 3 3

4 4 4

5 5 5

Name _____

Practice writing each numeral.

try these big numbers.

6 6 6

7 7 7

8 8 8

9 9 9

10 10 10

CD-3701

Name _____

Find the sums.

$$\begin{array}{r} 2 \\ + 2 \\ \hline \end{array}$$

$$\begin{array}{r} 1 \\ + 2 \\ \hline \end{array}$$

$$\begin{array}{r} 3 \\ + 1 \\ \hline \end{array}$$

$$\begin{array}{r} 1 \\ + 3 \\ \hline \end{array}$$

$$\begin{array}{r} 1 \\ + 1 \\ \hline \end{array}$$

CD-3701

Find the sums.

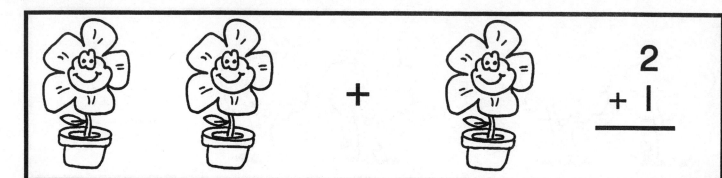

$$\begin{array}{r} 2 \\ + 1 \\ \hline \end{array}$$

$$\begin{array}{r} 2 \\ + 2 \\ \hline \end{array}$$

$$\begin{array}{r} 3 \\ + 1 \\ \hline \end{array}$$

$$\begin{array}{r} 1 \\ + 2 \\ \hline \end{array}$$

$$\begin{array}{r} 1 \\ + 3 \\ \hline \end{array}$$

CD-3701

Name _____ skill: learning the color red

Color the word and the pictures red.

1. Color the pictures red.

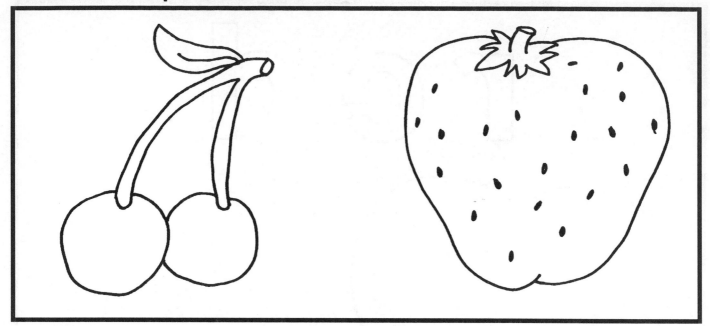

2. Draw a picture of something that is red.

69

CD-3701

Use a red crayon to color the pictures that are usually red.

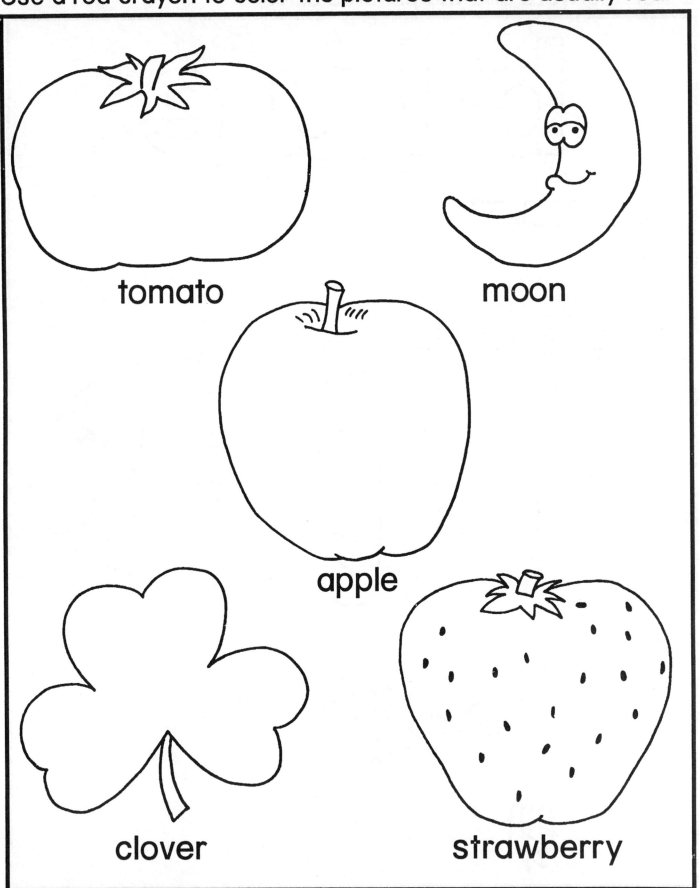

tomato

moon

apple

clover

strawberry

Name_____

skill: learning the color blue

Color the word and the pictures blue.

b l u e

71

CD-3701

1. Color the pictures blue.

2. Draw a picture of something that is blue.

skill: learning the color blue

Use a blue crayon to color the pictures that are usually blue.

water

tree

pear

blue jeans

cherries

CD-3701

Name _____ skill: learning the color orange

Color the word and the pictures orange.

74   CD-3701

1. Color the pictures orange.

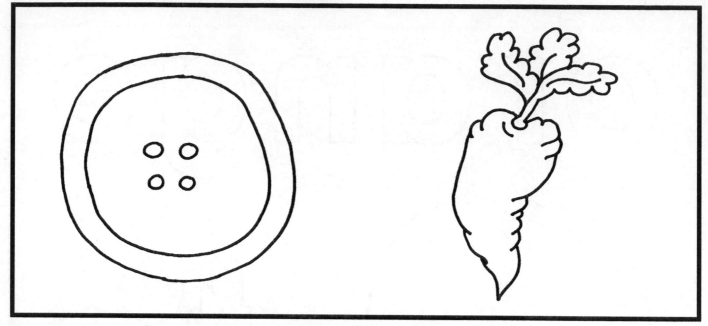

2. Draw a picture of something that is orange.

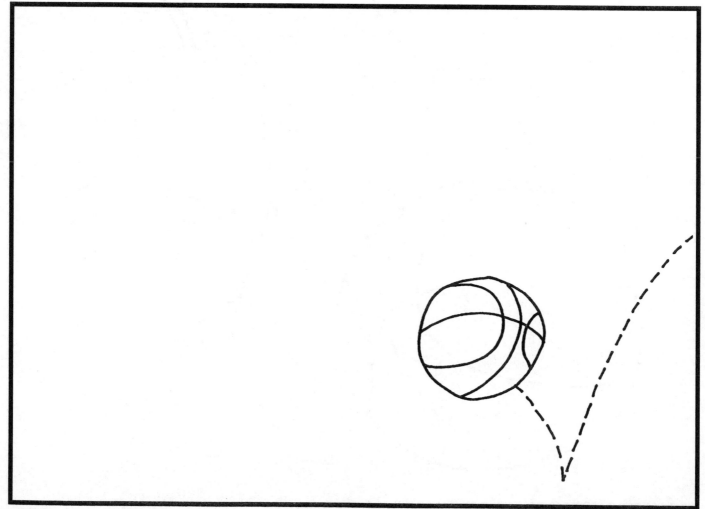

Use an orange crayon to color the pictures that are usually orange.

mushroom

pumpkin

basketball

igloo

orange

CD-3701

Name_____
Color the word and the pictures yellow.

yellow

77

CD-3701

1. Color the pictures yellow.

2. Draw a picture of something that is yellow.

CD-3701

Use a yellow crayon to color the pictures that
are usually yellow.

stop sign

sun

lemon

corn

leaf

Name_____
Color the word and the pictures green.

Use a green crayon to color the pictures that are usually green.

leaf

egg

camel

peas

tree

Color the word and the pictures brown.

b r o w n

Name _____

Use a brown crayon to color the pictures that are usually brown.

horse

bus

strawberry

puppy

football

CD-3701

Color the word and the pictures black.

Name_____

Use a black crayon to color the pictures that are usually black.

donut

hat

tire

pear

bat

CD-3701

Name_____ skill: learning the color pink

Color the word and the pictures pink.

p i n k

86 CD-3701

skill: color review-
red, blue, yellow

Trace over each word and color each picture.

red

blue

yellow

CD-3701

Trace over each word and color each picture.

green

purple

orange

CD-3701

Trace over each word and color each picture.

black

brown

gray

CD-3701

Name_____

skill: reading color words

Color each rain drop the correct color.

CD-3701

Color each piece of candy the correct color.

Name_____

Color each fish the correct color.

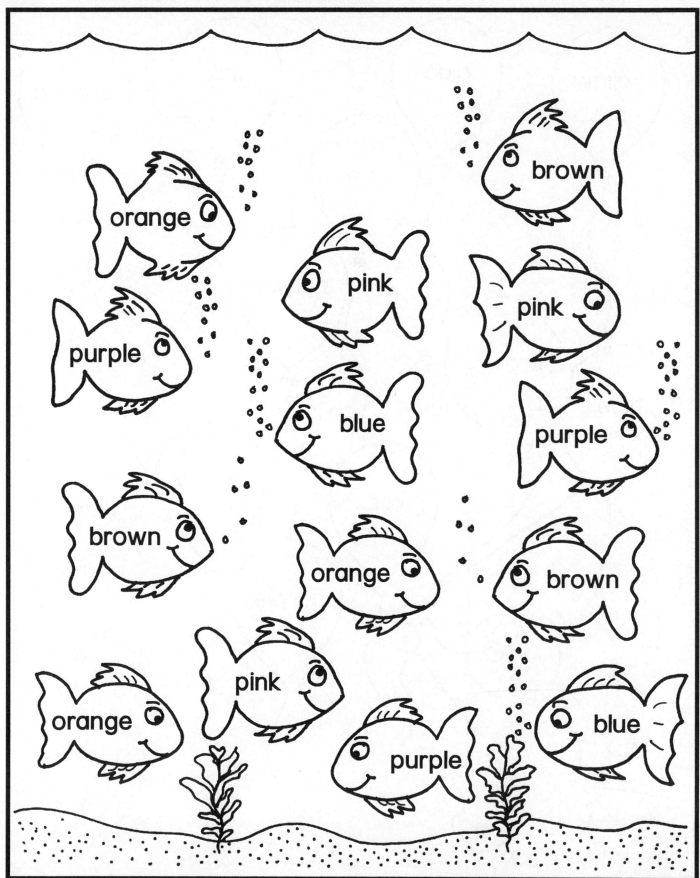

92   CD-3701

Name_____

Color each balloon the correct color.

Name_____

Color each star the correct color.

1. Trace over the circle and color it green.

skill: recognizing a circle
writing the word circle

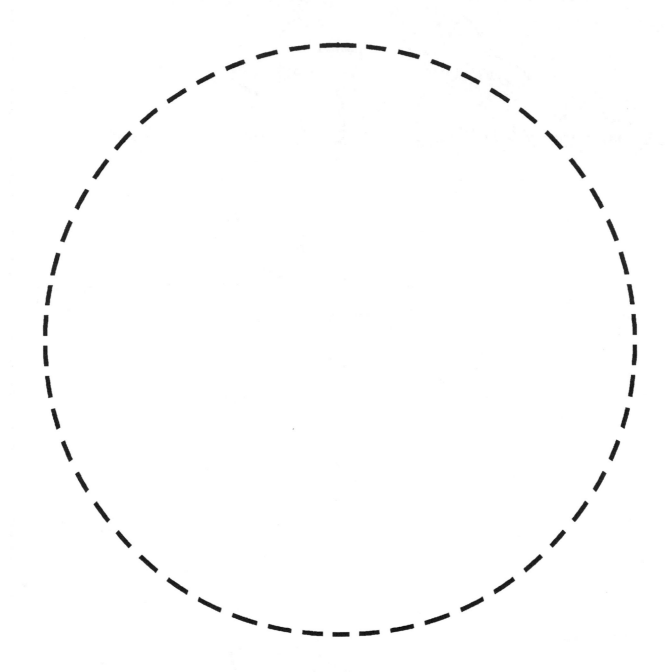

2. Practice writing the word "circle".

circle

CD-3701

Name_____
Trace and color all of the circles.

96   CD-3701

skill: recognizing a circle

Find and color all of the circles.

CD-3701

Cut out and paste the circles onto the correct spaces.

CD-3701

Name_____

1. Trace over the square and color it green.

2. Practice writing the word "square".

square

                   CD-3701

Name_____

Trace and color the squares.

Name_____

Find and color all of the squares.

Name_____   skill: recognizing a square
Follow the path of squares to get the camel to some water.

CD-3701

skill: recognizing a rectangle
writing the word rectangle

1. Trace over the rectangle and color it blue.

2. Practice writing the word "rectangle".

rectangle

103

Name_____

Trace and color the rectangles.

CD-3701

Name ____________________ skill: recognizing rectangle

Color each space purple if it has a

CD-3701

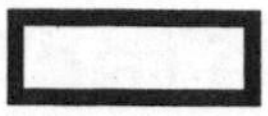

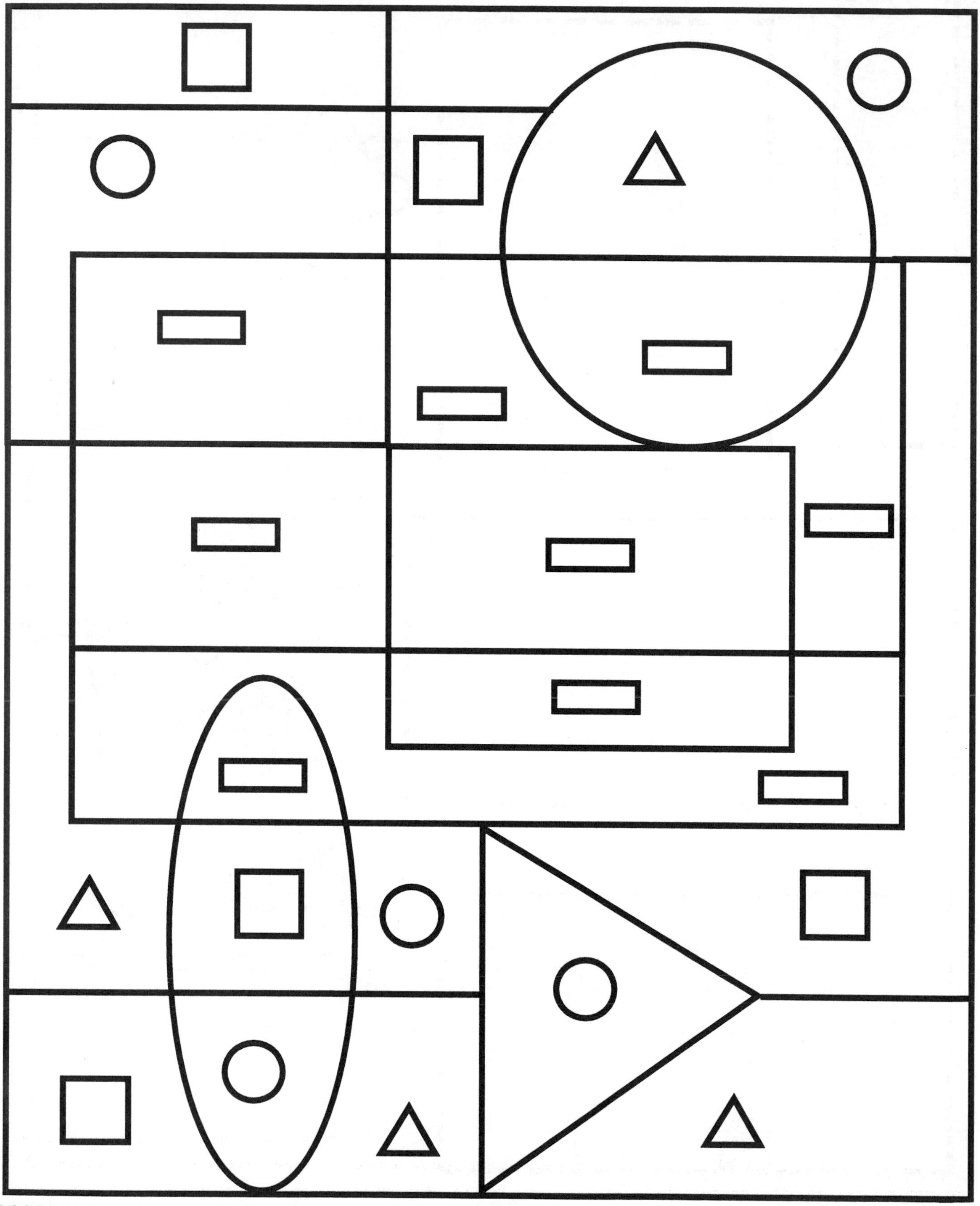

Name_____

Find and color all of the rectangles.

CD-3701

Name_____

1. Trace over the triangle and color it yellow.

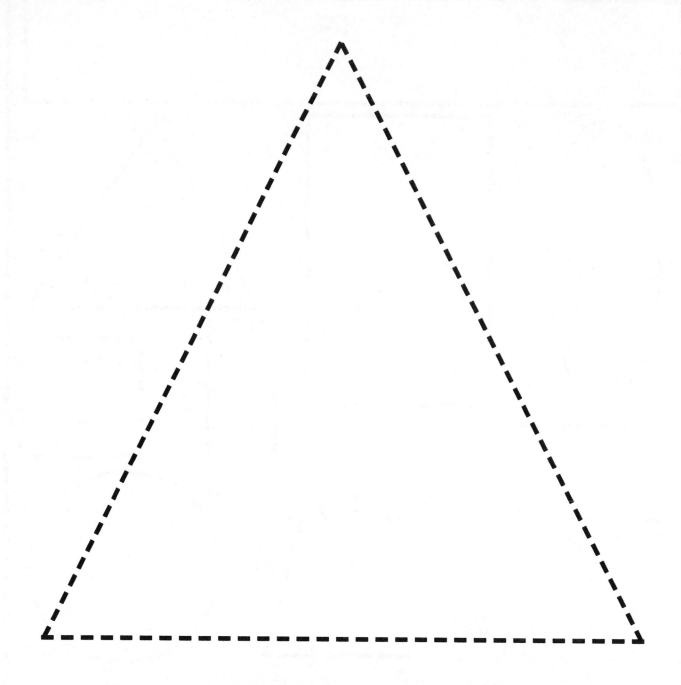

2. Practice writing the word "triangle".

triangle

Name_____
Trace and color the triangles.

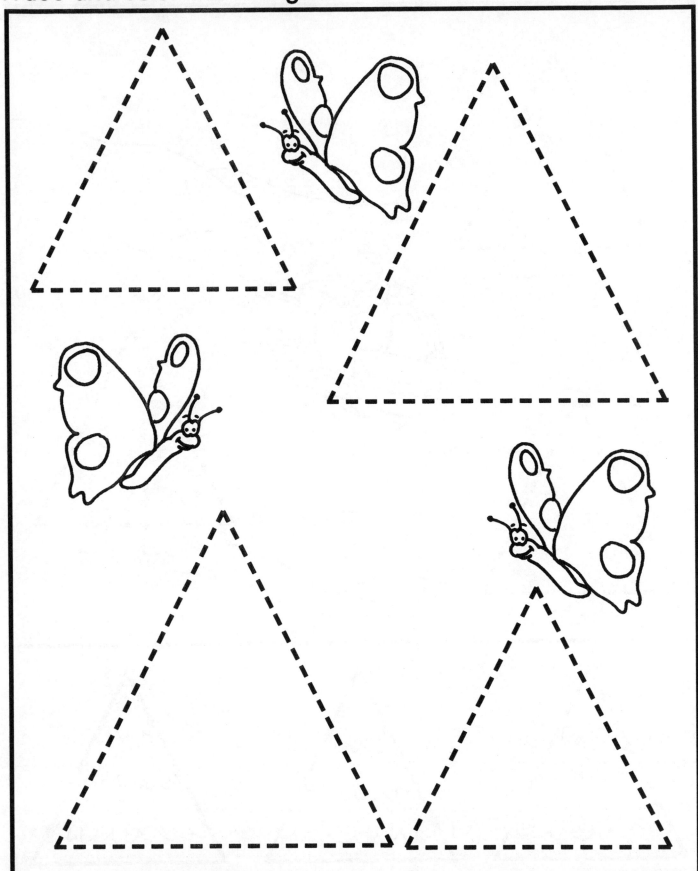

Name_____

✂ Cut out and paste the triangles onto the correct spaces.

CD-3701

Name_____

Find and color the triangles.

CD-3701

Draw a line to match the shapes that are alike.

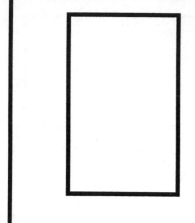
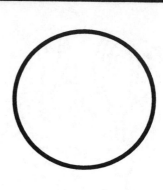
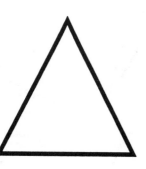

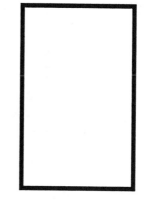
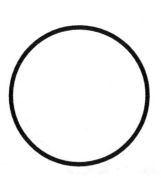
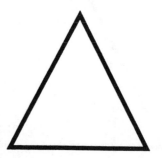

CD-3701

Name_____

Color the shapes. Use the color key.

◯ = red   ▯ = yellow

▢ = blue   △ = green

112   CD-3701

Name ____________________

skill: shapes review square, circle, triangle, rectangle

In each box draw the correct shape and write the word.

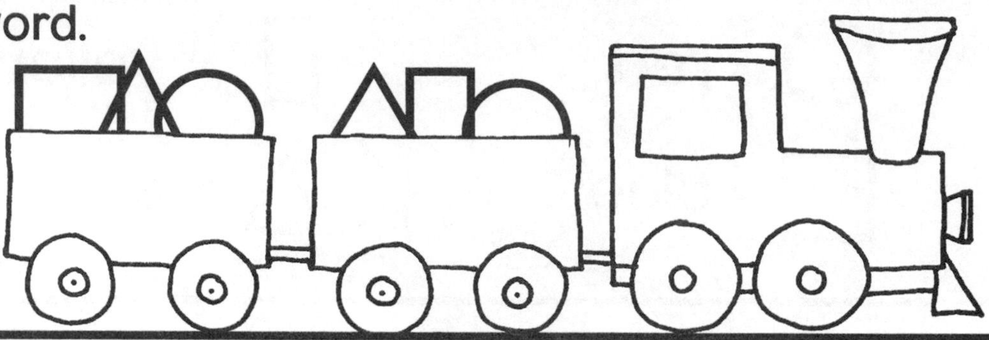

square

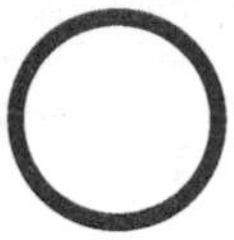

circle

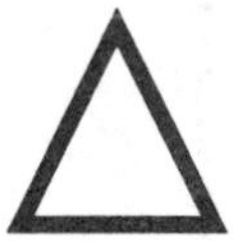

triangle

rectangle

Name_____

1. Trace over the heart and color it red.

2. Practice writing the word "heart".

heart

Trace and color the hearts.

115 CD-3701

Name_____

1. Trace over the diamond and color it red.

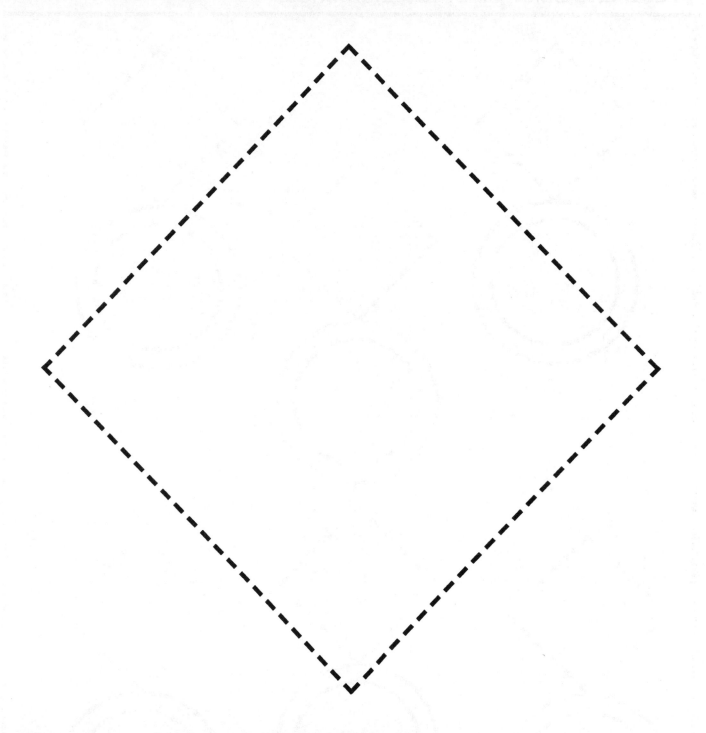

2. Practice writing the word "diamond".

diamond

116

Name_____

Trace and color all of the diamonds.

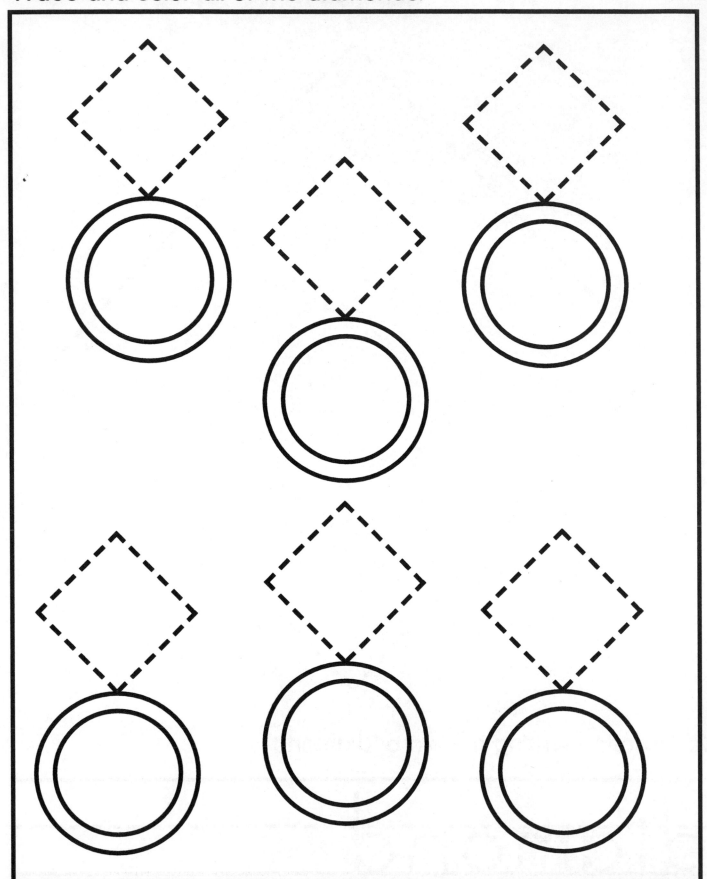

CD-3701

Name_____

1. Trace over the oval and color it pink.

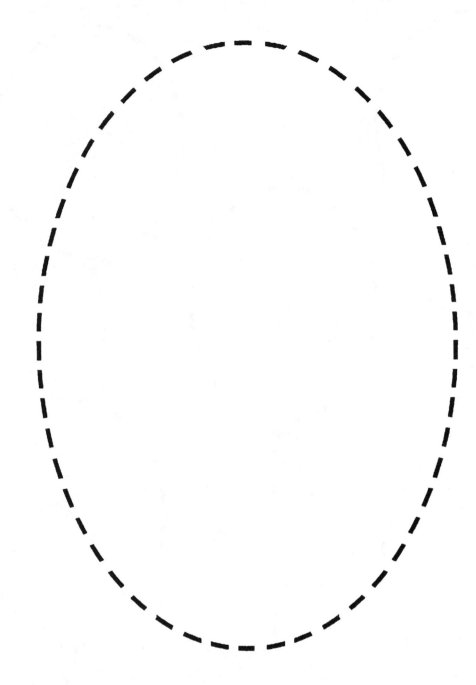

2. Practice writing the word "oval".

oval

skill: tracing ovals

Trace and color all of the ovals.

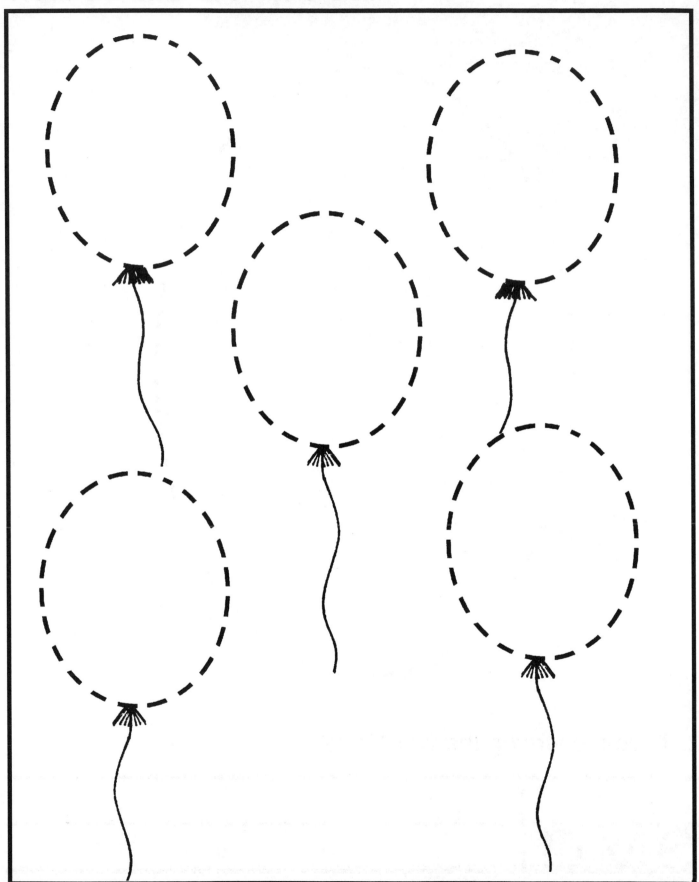

119

Name_____

skill: recognizing a star
writing the word star

1. Trace over the star and color it orange.

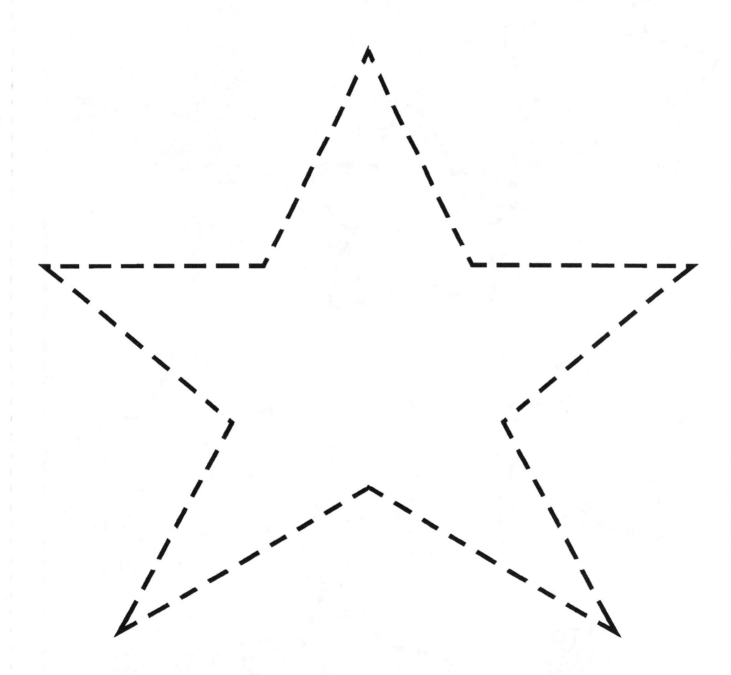

2. Practice writing the word "star".

star

120

CD-3701

Trace and color all of the stars.

skill: tracing stars

121

CD-3701

Name_____

In each box draw the correct shape and write the word.

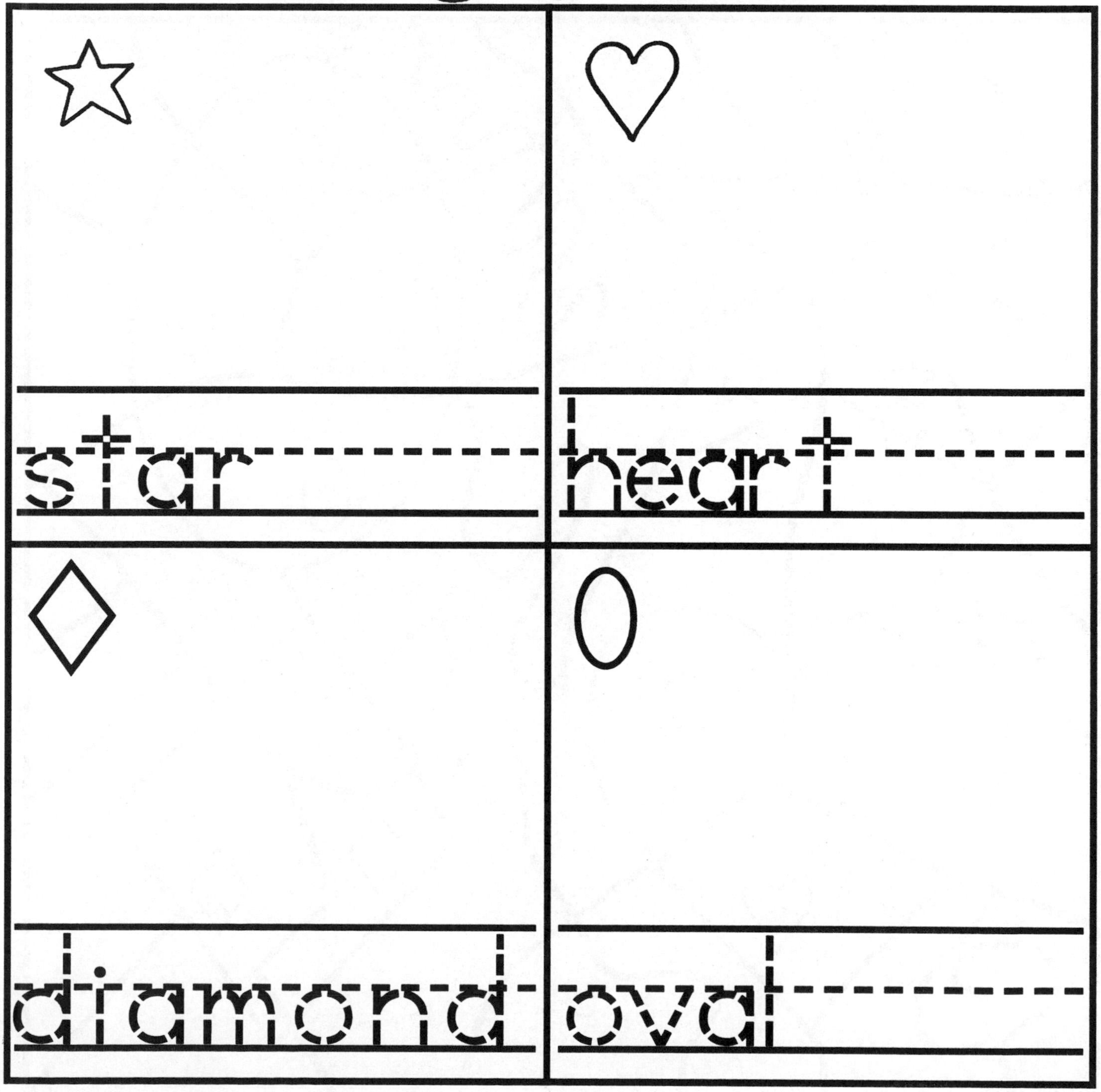

☆

★ star

♡

heart

◇

diamond

O

oval

122   CD-3701

Name_____

Color the spaces. Use the color key.

☆ = red   ◇ = blue   ⬭ = green   ♡ = yellow

123   CD-3701

Name_____

In each box trace the shape then draw another shape like the first one.

CD-3701

Alphabet Award

_____

receives this award for

_____

Keep up the great work!

_____   _____
signed   date

I Know My Colors!

_____

receives this award for

_____

Great Job!

_____   _____
signed   date

★ Numbers Award ★

_____

receives this award for

_____

Keep up the great work!

_____ _____
signed   date

I Know My Shapes

_____

receives this award for

_____

Great Job!

_____ _____
signed   date

                                   CD-3701

I
Know The
Alphabet!

Star
Student!

We are proud of you!

_____

deserves this award for

_____

Keep up the great work!

_____   _____

signed   date

127   CD-3701